The Girl Singer

The Girl Singer

POEMS

Marianne Worthington

**FIRESIDE
INDUSTRIES**

Published by Fireside Industries
An imprint of the University Press of Kentucky

Editorial and Sales Offices: The University Press of Kentucky
663 South Limestone Street, Lexington, Kentucky 40508-4008
www.kentuckypress.com

Cataloging-in-Publication data available from the Library of Congress

ISBN 978-1-950564-18-7 (hardcover : acid-free paper)
ISBN 978-1-950564-19-4 (paperback : acid-free paper)
ISBN 978-1-950564-20-0 (pdf)
ISBN 978-1-950564-21-7 (epub)

This book is printed on acid-free paper meeting
the requirements of the American National Standard
for Permanence in Paper for Printed Library Materials.

Manufactured in the United States of America.

for Keith & Katelyn,
and for Haroldine & Tom in memoriam

In all the world there is nothing braver than the heart of a singing bird. Can you think what it means to be so small and so beautiful in a world full of guns and traps, of cats and hawks, of crafty snakes and crows and squirrels and bluejays all of whom rob the nest,— and yet to sing and sing again that all nature is good, is good!

Emma Bell Miles, *Our Southern Birds*, 1919

Contents

II

III

The Girl Singer

Rank Stranger

Storm clouds and lashing rain follow
me out of the Jewel City alongside
the words of the poet who claimed

her grandmother lived such old ways
it was as if all time had stopped,
like she had jammed *her thorn broom*

handle into the world's axis. Still,
the Ohio River curls on as I hit
the highway toward home. The road

is a smoldering ribbon past the oil
refineries in Ashland. The green
and lavender hills smear in the opening

ahead as the sun raises the cruel curtain
of haze and reveals a colony of turkey
buzzards by the roadside. Their feathers

glisten dark jewels, their shoulders droop.
I see the stiff legs of the dead
thing they are encircling. They join

the one already atop the dead,
the one glutting from the side,
the others waiting their turn.

I

Index of Canticles

A. P. Carter v. Sara Carter, 1932

Her voice was deep as Copper Creek—
rough as the white oak on Clinch Mountain;
she was singing something lonesome,
leaves sifting the sound,
floated down like I
had to find it and my mission: to doctor songs;
and follow a black man through
all the places I couldn't go, closed up to me
wary, guarded—I walked the tracks toward
a life of music and Sara, prettier than
the songs. Again, I left my mother,

Heard me singing "Lonesome Valley"
name like the place where we lived;
heard me singing while he was selling fruit trees
swaying me to think it was me he
wanted, but it wasn't. No,
he wanted me and Maybelle to traipse
all over creation dragging our babies around
like guitar cases. Finally, I said
the plain truth: I love Coy Bayes better than
anything I ever laid eyes on. I left
the songs, left my children.

Goodbye Poor Valley

I couldn't stop searching for that sound.

I never could make anybody understand.

Dead Man's Tuning

Timberman, wielding an ax, a drunkard
who yelled and hit? I can only concoct you,
Grandfather, for no one will say what you
really were. Your photographs are mock-ups
of my father and sister: crooked nose,
brow turned firm over eyes bluer than steel.
This much I know from what little I know:
Your fiddle bow scraped through blistering days

like a crosscut saw through hardwood—*Sourwood
Mountain, Woodchopper's Breakdown, Temperance Reel*—
your singing voice was coarse and high, an echo
lumbers through this dream I had: You're teaching
George Harrison to play your banjolele
both of you grinning and stomping your feet!

Strings

A girl in Tennessee hears
her uncle fiddle

through his nights. Jigs
and reels riff

in her ears and stick.
The uncle gifts her a mandolin.

She fingers the neck,
takes the open fifths

into the choir of her heart.
She learns the strings, first

strumming and plucking
then brushing and picking.

They vibrate, then ring,
sing back to the campfires

in Romania, back to suppers
of lamb and mint, back

to the baby dozing
as her father unwraps

a cobza and casts out
a tune for the rising moon.

Knoxville Boy

Oh Willie dear don't kill me here
I'm unprepared to die
        "Knoxville Girl," Appalachian murder ballad

Son, I said, what have you done?
He came in late, my boy, his shirt front
and britches muddy and stained.
How come that blood on your shirt sleeve?

I put the light on to see his face,
our shadows stretched up the stairwell
wall, our silhouettes as slow as night.
He told me to go back to bed,

says, Mother, I've just got
one of those bad headaches
that makes my nose bleed. Says fetch
me some aspirin and a cold wash

rag. Something about the way
he smelled put me in mind
of that dark-eyed girl he's been
seeing. One of those Happy Holler

girls works over at the Standard
Knitting Mills, had a little girl, not
a soul knows who its daddy was,
and when my boy started

going with that girl, seems
like a pall covered his face, his eyes

dull as the Tennessee River. Next
thing I knew, the sheriff beat

on the door and wanted in, says
there's been a killing on the river
bank. I looked up the stairs
to my fair boy, *Oh Willie*

dear what have we done?
My son come tell it to me.

Recitatives on a Murder
(Wilkes County, North Carolina, 1866)

I. ANN FOSTER MELTON SPEAKS FROM HER DEATHBED

It's true, yes, I had married James
but Tom and me, we could not quit.
We'd been as one since that morning

Mommy found us abed together.
Now the only thing left to do
is turn my face toward the wall.

Young Laurie Foster's chestnut locks
and blithe blue eyes are vexing me.
I told my man and all the girls

who gathered round me in the end
the truth. I could not bear to see
Laurie and Tom Dula carry on.

We plunged the knife into her ribs.
We beat her head until she bled.
I knew they would not hang me here.

They said my neck was just too fair
to stretch the hemp. Men could not look
at me and keep their heads. A man

in Wilkes told me my face was sweeter
than he'd seen. Tonight I dream
my hair is still coal black, my skin

as white as milk. Now do you hear
that hiss of steam, like spring water
doused on hot rocks? And can you see

the flames of hell dancing round me?
A bed afire will make a ring
and bring me back to Tom. He waits

for me beside our river spot.
I see his sweet head hanging down
while the devil plays Tom's fiddle.

I took my fiddle to the War.
Because I wasn't but 17
they made me troop musician.

The fiddle kept the men at ease
and helped me recollect the pure
path of gals pacing for me back

home—Fosters all—Laurie, Ann, Perlene.
Lord, sometimes I saw the trouble
bubbling just like the river

at Yadkin Falls. I've rubbed them all
there on the bank. Laurie's dark hair
smells rich as wood smoke, and Annie's

little feet fit right in my hand,
her neck so handsome it takes your breath.
Perlene, my God, her waist, her breasts

shapely and high, a sight to see
and she's as sporty as a fox.
What would I do if forced to choose?

One bloody morning in late May
the answer to that question came.
I buried Laurie. I had to,

which made me guilty of the crime
of murder. I hid her shoes,
her father's mare. I took the blame

and swore the oath: Was only me
who had a hand in Laurie's death.
But at the gallows they asked again.

Men! I say, *do you see this hand?*
I never even harmed a hair
on poor sweet Laura Foster's head!

I told Laurie's daddy I'd look
for his mare if he'd give me a
quart of whiskey. Hateful old fool,

he only cared about that horse.
I knew that Laurie had it bad
at home, not a pot to piss in.

We were cousins to each other,
me and Laurie and Annie, and
we each one had our turn with Tom.

But it was me would do to Tom
what other women wouldn't dare.
He told me once I was his vixen,

and I would swear a lie for Tom.
But now all four of us had it—
the syphilis—and Tom was vexed.

But me and Ann was stuck in jail—
that nasty jailer with no teeth,
the food so foul we could not eat—

yet I began to see that Ann
would never get the first degree
because them men they put such store

in her good looks and even though
the deputies had heard me brag
I'd done the deed, I testified

for the State. They convicted Tom.
Me and Annie we went back home.
A sister brought Tom's body back.

He rests beside the Yadkin shore
where crabapples bear fruit so sour
the songbirds stay out of the trees.

IV. LAURA FOSTER SPEAKS FROM THE GRAVE

Tom brought me blossoms from his trees
all in the merry month of May
when me and Tom was set to wed.

I double-dressed and bundled
the rest, lit out for the river
bank. I didn't care to leave old

Pa and Happy Valley, although
I felt a queer sadness taking
Pa's mare. Soon I saw Tom coming

through the sweet birch and the dogwoods,
their flowers already past peak.
I thought I saw a shadow cross

Tom's face—he wore no hat that day—
but it must have been the sunlight
slipping through the woods like me.

Tom reached and hugged me down to him,
then begged to be excused. I joked
about his insides turned to water,

then he plumb vanished like a haint
behind a stand of black oak trees.
Upon my head I felt a blow,

the burn of blade inside my heart.
Before I fell and drifted off
I heard the laughter of Perlene

(or was it Annie?) warp and coil
around the trees, sway in the air
like a robber from the gallows.

They didn't find me for three months.
Time enough to roam these hills,
time enough to find my voice.

The Girl Singer

How hard it was to hold my body against
defeat and come to be known as just a girl

singer by those men who said *we're doing
you a big favor, honey.* Once, I sang the lonely

songs I loved. The A-minor chord on my black
Gibson hummed lonesome as a grave. I strummed

right through their promises *Crying O!
the dreadful wind and the rain.* On stage I was

one notch below the gap-toothed hayseed
in his checkered jacket and short pants clowning

around with me as his sidekick and we'd laugh
and laugh. *I dug on your grave the better*

part of last night. Too sorrowful, they said. The bosses
heard enough about sick-hearted boys chasing

aggravating beauties, poor orphan children dropping
and dying in the snow. War was over, they said.

Be old-fashioned but not too much. How hard
it was to fetch my voice for chirpier songs.

Oh the cuckoo, she never hollers coo-coo. I wore
down. I mourned the women killed in all the murder

ballads I knew—bludgeoned-stabbed-drowned-floated
downstream to the miller's cove. *He made fiddle screws*

from her little finger bones. I had to quit singing our songs.
Her clothes all wet and muddy they laid her on a plank.

Barn Dance (Road Show)

Hungry as she was for fame
she never thought they'd change

her name or dress her up
in homely cloth and make

her say those scripted jokes.
She never thought she'd have to ride

the waves of heat all summer long
to hawk the barn dance radio

in close school halls and fairground tents.
No one said she'd bear alone

the blues, the cramps, the damp-filled nights,
the silhouettes on hotel walls

where her name in secret
she would write in letters of bright gold.

She couldn't know the sacrifice
to sing the lonely songs she loved

would be rough travel with quarrelsome
men who never guessed her given name

and didn't give a damn anyway.

Barn Dance (Costume)

Reject the lace petticoats, the rickrack
hems. Reject the gingham bonnet's

stranglehold, the myth of calico
for modesty's sake. Forsake

the man whispering backstage
your fate, his eyes green

as dollar bills. Kick off
your lace-up boots and ankle

skirts and wail the blue notes
that howl your heart's longing. Hop

high and belt out the one about
my Lulu Gal wearing that red dress

from the railroad man and those shoes
from a driver in the mines. Stay

in the pit with the rough and the rowdy.
Hop high! Don't look behind.

Barn Dance (Chorus)

Little Darlin's not my name
   Cathy Fink

It's not cousin, gal, honey, or sweetheart.
Not little miss, little maid, little jo,

little shoe, little sunbonnet. Our names
aren't sister, girl, lady, or aunt. Listen.

We had to play like one of the boys—cards,
drinking, jokes—to hold our own on radio,

at whistlestops, barn dances, schoolhouses,
church meetings, and every blazing county

fair in all the states they used for our names:
Montana, Louisiana, Texas.

Don't call us bluebird, songbird, nightingale,
cricket. Not sunshine, moonshine, violet,

or sugar. Not brown eyes, black-eyed susie,
daisy, or laughin' lindy. Listen. If you want

us, say the names our mothers gave us.
Recall how we really were: rawboned,

standing spraddle-legged while we
headlined those mean stages.

Barn Dance
(Cousin Emmy Remembers Her Show Car)

My brother-in-law always drove the show
car, knew how to navigate every pig

track and back road without a map, could drive
safe in cities, too. Drop us at the load

out on time without a hitch. Cheerful he
was, and good hearted, a big grin to match

his wit. But Lord, he had enough of South
Knoxville still in him to park that show car

at a tilt under Mam's old shed and prop
the door open, let his hunting dogs flop

in the back like a doghouse. So if you
were to come up on it, see that Cadillac

full of old yellow dogs, you'd think we were
right trashy. He kept the car shined up for us

and always tried to clean the seats
but we were forever brushing dog hair

from each other's hind ends before a gig,
blonde swirls and hanks we picked like strings,

had to strum off quick
as a drop thumb on the banjo.

Maybelle Carter on Singing Hillbilly Boogie with Sara, ca. 1963

April in California and a dry wind hollers from the Great Basin,
not like home where the redbud and dogwood are flashing

in full sun and the mountains smell green even at night.
I have been revived in middle age. These boys want us to make

one more record, so when we stop at Sara's, we just assume
our places like it's 1927 again. We both sit in her ladder-

back dining room chairs. We both have guitars today.
What has changed? The Carter Scratch is our path

to home. I thumb-pick a hot run and my ripe old maple
guitar vibrates against my belly. Sara thrums a rhythm

fixed as the years since we were girls in Maces Spring.
We lower the key. Sara mourns out the lead and I echo

back the refrain. Old blues, solemn as a stain but fast,
we take it so fast. We are pitched to a pacific run

to beat the truth coming at the end of the line—
I'll be gone long gone someday 'fore long.

On Seeing a Letter Patsy Cline Wrote to Nudie the Tailor

Her handwriting sways like a song
   in dull pencil on dime store tablet paper.
     The rodeo tailor's name is misspelled

but other details are exact: her bust
   measurements, her waist, her hips.
     A real woman's shape will swing

toward the microphone, in the silver
   cape lined in red satin she's asking
     the tailor to make. Yearning and ache

will glitter her voice as a flash
   comes. She remembers the red
     cowgirl suit sewn by her mother,

wagon wheels and rhinestones burden
   the hem. The tailor receives her letter
     as the wreckage smolders nose-first

in the murky woods. *How long will it take you?*
   she asks the tailor. Forever we search
     for the spangle and sequin.

Forever we follow her calligraphed tones.

Rebel Girl (Hazel Dickens)

As if all the world's wrongs had come to sit in her throat,
she wandered the Baltimore streets where the boardinghouse

signs warned those like her looking for factory work: *No Dogs
or Hillbillies.* She settled in Little Appalachia amid her rough

refugees who journeyed north when the mines mechanized,
the coal bosses commanding the mountains stripped and gutted.

She dug her way in, unearthed her voice, the one
she had used back home when her daddy would call her out

to sing for neighbors. But now there was a misery in her melodies,
a bad taste she chased with words that cut to the truth like the coal

seams her brothers laid bare in the mines. *If you can't stand
by me, don't stand in my way.* Her rawness split hearts open,

her tunes hypnotized sickness and beat back grief and lack.
She bellowed down mean men, murderers, union busters.

People quit making fun of the hillbilly in her talk
and celebrated the worker, the fallen, the bereaved.

I saw Bobby Bare kiss Marty Stuart

on the stage of the Ryman after Bobby had played
"Marie Laveau" and "That's How I Got to Memphis"

and "Detroit City" and my friend who's a music manager
whispered to me that Bobby Bare was the sweetest man

in Nashville and his voice was pitch perfect at age 78
and he still wore washed out jeans and a white hat

and a sloppy overshirt and no shit or horsing around
on stage just straight ahead music so that by the time

it was over and he kissed Marty Stuart goodbye
I was crying but I was on the verge anyway being

at the Ryman where my parents stopped
on their honeymoon one October night in 1952

and saw Ernest Tubb and Little Jimmy Dickens
and Minnie Pearl and I didn't know the Ryman stage

was so small but the Grand Ole Opry Square
Dancers had just clogged in a corner of that little

stage in their red checkered outfits and white tap
shoes and I felt the same homesickness I felt the first

time I saw *Coal Miner's Daughter* and Ted says
to Clary Get up Mommy do your dance and she does

and I'm the only one in the theatre weeping
at what most people thought was hokey and hillbilly

but it made me miss the old TV shows that broadcast
into my parents' den every Saturday afternoon and we

all quit what we were doing to watch Lester & Earl
and Teddy & Doyle & Loretta and Porter & Pretty Miss

Norma Jean & later Dolly and my daddy would holler
into the kitchen for my mother to come out to the den

and look here at Ole Possum or Charley Pride or
Wilma Lee & Stoney Cooper singing "Walking

My Lord up Calvary's Hill" and when the credits
rolled on *The Wilburn Brothers Show* Loretta kicked

off her shoes and danced her Mommy's dance
in her stocking feet and I tell you I lived

for that on Saturdays until one time in 1973 Daddy
stood up from his TV watching chair and yelled

for all of us to come running quick and look here
at this little feller picking the mandolin with Lester

Flatt's new band on Porter Wagoner's show and we
grouped around the Zenith and gaped at Marty Stuart's

wizardry and I fell dead in love with him
that very moment and now here we are forty years

later and he's reinvented that template of old country
music TV shows with an opening hit, a comic, a guest

or two, the girl singer, and hymn time and invites all
his old friends and shepherds the young unknowns

the way Lester still shepherds him and they all play
at his annual late night jam and fireworks blazed

above the Ryman before we went into the show
and Marty stood on stage three straight hours

in his black frock coat nodding his wild shock
of hair back and forth and tapping his boot

and then he brought out his mommy and made
her tell all about her new book of photographs

and before we knew it the Mavericks were burning
down the house with "All You Ever Do Is Bring

Me Down" then Marty asks Raul Malo to sing
a birthday song to Manuel the glitter tailor

who is also on stage because Marty honors all parts
of country music even costumes and Raul sings

Don Gibson's "I'd Be a Legend in My Time" and I cry
even harder because once when I was a kid we saw

Don Gibson in the K-Mart when he lived in Knoxville
in a beat up trailer on Clinton Highway and had seen

better days but Mother had all his records and then
when I think I can't cry any more Marty says

they are all going upstairs after the show to shake
and howdy with anyone who wants to meet them

and have their picture made and sometimes it's 4 a.m.
before they can leave the Ryman but I am

too embarrassed to admit how much I love
Marty and his wife Connie Smith and now Hilda

his mommy and don't want to make a fan fool
of myself so we step out into the late night and watch

the crowd leave and listen to people converse
in German and Spanish and maybe Bengali and I

realize they too love this exceptionally long musical
that crosses decades and languages and has carried

us to Nashville where the noisy streets are still
teeming with girls in Western boots and boys

in Western shirts and music blares out of every bar
we pass on Broadway and lifts us into the night's

cacophony and even when we get back home
and even now I can't stop crying

I Will Always Love You

My mother lifts her new Kodak Brownie
8 mm from its copper suitcase. *Come on,*
we're going to town. At the grand

opening of the Fountain City Esso
local politicians glad-hand
and cut the ribbon. All my favorite

local singers are here: the Brewster Brothers,
Danny Bailey & Gloria Bell, Red & Fred,
and a girl from Locust Ridge named

Dolly. Mother flips up the viewfinder,
squints and aims while traffic roars
down Broadway behind us

and Dolly, dressed in a homemade
jumper, sings high and pure
Don't let me cross over love's cheating line.

Weeks pass before I see the mute images
unspool onto the wall of our darkened den,
hear only the two-toned hum

of the projector, the percussion of the film
clacking into the empty reel. Our truncated
story plays out like a dream: black bear

cubs in the Smokies, a Sunday School
party in my aunt's basement, Norris Lake,
Dolly Parton, my mean cousin getting

a whipping, two old women in black
dresses sitting on a porch. Their hands
are liver-spotted, gnarled, entwined.

Love in the Cold War

My parents traveled from Knoxville to Nashville for their honeymoon
to see the Saturday night music show at the Mother Church.
Little Jimmy Dickens sang "They Locked God Outside the Iron
    Curtain."
My father misunderstood the refrain: *They locked John where?* he
    asked.

To see the Saturday night music show at the Mother Church
they sat in the hot sanctuary on wooden pews but
my father misunderstood the refrain: *John got locked up where?*
while Ernest Tubb electrified the cathedral walking that floor.

In the hot sanctuary they sat on wooden pews,
the music of their youth personified in Nudie suits and steel guitars,
Ernest Tubb electrifying the cathedral walking that floor.
They were new lovers holding one life to stand on country songs.

The music of their youth personified in Nudie suits and steel guitars,
the twang and beat of the honky-tonk 4/4 Shuffle,
these new lovers held one life to stand on country songs
while Ray Price's "Crazy Arms" lifted them over the moist heavy air.

The twang and beat of the honky-tonk 4/4 Shuffle,
Little Jimmy Dickens singing "They Locked God Outside the Iron
    Curtain"
and Ray Price's "Crazy Arms" lifting them over the moist heavy air
when my parents traveled from Knoxville to Nashville for their
    honeymoon.

Poem in My Grandmother's Voice

Jesus died for your sins. What
do you reckon he would say
about that miniskirt and go-go boots
you're fixing to wear to church?

Pentecost 1965

First Creek churns under the 5th Avenue
viaduct in the old part of town. Brick
warehouses testify to a Sunday
shifting toward a lazy haze. Summer is coming.

The girl watches for the Acts Man riding
his bicycle down Central Avenue. He's duct-
taped plastic sheets to dowels, built a shelter
so he can ride in all weathers. She likes
to read his hand-scrawled signs fixed to his bike-
tent, verses from the Acts of the Apostles.

At church the preacher *could* call him a witness
for Jesus, but the Acts Man is black and poor,
ignored, even though we all see him every day.
He peddles down Magnolia Avenue like it's the road
to Damascus. The preacher cries about tongues
of fire and a mighty rushing wind, but the green
branches sway easy when the Acts Man passes.

After church the girl's great feast will be killed
lettuce and onions, sidemeat and skillet
cornbread set atop a Formica table.
And when the Day of Pentecost was fully come,
they were all with one accord in one place.

The only way out

was for the kids to crawl
    under the supper table packed
        with family in our tiny red
Formica kitchen
    but I stayed behind with
        the Boston terrier waiting

below for crumbs of talk
    I'm not supposed to hear—
        drunkard, asshole, divorce,

the words damping
    through vinyl and chrome
        juddering in my ears.

My Grandmother's Sewing Notions

Jaybirds near her window were pure
aggravation. She sent my cousins

scrambling up sugar maples to tear
down their nests, a nickel apiece.

Who could fathom her riotous days?
Noise, like a vapor, overwhelmed

her. *Hush,* she'd say. Hush *now.*
She ordered quiet to locate

one unflawed pearl button inside
her rusting button can, the matching

thread, her seam ripper, hooks and eyes.

Once

She lived with her child in two damp rooms, shared
a bed. Loneliness cloaked day after day of routine.

When the dog died, she dug a pillowslip from cool
linen shelves, prayed he would not bloat in the heat

before she got him in the ground. Shoveling
beneath the stand of black locusts, she set

her mouth like a stone against howling.

Vocal School

My grandmother never shuts up even though her declarations
are lost to the ether so long ago. She had a hitch and quaver

in her chatter like a flickering light. Once in my father's last confusions
he tried to tell me a story about a cousin who had done something

funny but couldn't remember the punchline. He gave up, his voice
a tremble: *I can't recall. You'll have to get Pearl to tell it.*

I knew then he was lost although he recalled his dead mother's name
and held to the filament of her voice until his end. Often I dream

her talking in the rooms of her roomy house. Pearl paring Red
Delicious apples in the kitchen and speaking of recitations

they had to give in school. One time, her classmate was unprepared
for his turn but stood up anyway to try and make his sentence:

Earl Hunt were tall and gangly, he said. The unfitting verb
made her laugh. Then she was sorry, her voice switching dim.

That boy got the belt and sent to stand in the corner. I turn
my face to the wall like that boy in a cold schoolroom

in east Tennessee. I recite the iridescence of her name
in the dark, willing the pitch of her voice to channel my dreams.

War Story

The little boy loves his grandfather even though
the old man harbors a circle of hate in his heart
as red and round as the Japanese flag.

The grandfather will not buy the church
a new piano, even though he can, because the church
wants a Yamaha or a Kawai. There's a committee.

The boy wants to learn to play the piano more
than baseball, more than He-Man, more than girls.
A woman in the church could give him lessons

but *not on no damn jap piano*, the grandfather
says, as if the keys were ground from bones,
as if the strings were cut from guts, as if
the harp might echo his screams.

Minor Detour through an Old Knoxville Neighborhood

The apartment complex at Arbor Place where I shared
a one-bedroom with my cousin bears the derelict

face of abuse. Doors and windows missing or kicked
in expose the shadows of a few squatters, their abandoned

eyes. Ruin stings my throat. What happened
to my old street where half a block away the bungalows

rooted in manicured lawns like oaks and inside one
I studied piano with a gentle man who stood behind

me and pushed my shoulders down and said *breathe here*
and *pianissimo* and *rubato* while I played my *Raindrop Prelude?*

James Brown Performs "Cold Sweat" on *American Bandstand*, 1968

We were practicing our splits, perfecting our slides
across the basement floor on one foot, impossible
to beat the hardest working man in show business
even as we cheated in our sock feet. Upstairs,
our grandmother hurled her wrecking-ball voice
at us before we finished miming the first verse—

       I don't care *ha!* about your past

We knew she wasn't really hollering about the TV blaring
or that we'd skipped our Saturday housework chores.
She wasn't really cross that we dragged her white
chenille bedspread downstairs so we'd have a royal
robe to throw off at the end of the song. We twisted
against the timbre of her rage, while we mimicked Soul
Brother No. 1 cloaked by Danny Ray then coaxed
off the stage exhausted only to revive, abandon
the cape, grab that microphone and whirl
                  and gyrate and split
                       us one more time.

Slow Dance

I hear the meter of my father's gait,
his walker clattering through the hallway;
then, a rest, while he pauses for a breath.
His withered leg and foot disobey like
an errant child lagging behind. We bend
and lift his limbs so he can sit to watch
ball games, outfielders leaping for the catch.

Every morning he leans against the sink,
looks out the kitchen window for yellow
buses hauling children or for the trash
men. He studies the neighbor boy, chest thrust
into the yawning mouth of his pickup.
I used to adjust my timing, he says,
then turns to start his noisy waltz again.

Corvus

My mother works the crossword while we wait
for my father to die. I imagine
his father, with his pretty fiddle, his
hateful temper, standing on death's logging
road to meet his son. My daughter's nightgowns
flutter forgotten on the clothesline.
In sleep, she is my mother reborn.
Ready or not, our days begin on black

wings and end the same. The crows strut and squawk
their dim song. Caw! is a three-letter word
for mockery. Into our yard they come
marching like drunken soldiers. Mother hates
this murder but feeds them stale bread, knowing
they steal our brightest treasures for their nests.

Thanksgiving Eve

My mother sleeps in my bed,
my father sleeps

in a ground starting to freeze.
I wake in a moonlit room

not meant for sleeping.
What else to do but let go

of his starched pajamas folded
to rest, the wheelchairs

and walkers, the cornucopia
of plastic urinals in my closets.

Herons on the Holston

I lift myself to see one alone on the shore
        as I channel my car in the back parking lot. My mother
            has settled here, a rest home squatting
                heavy near the raw edge of a river in a forgotten
                    part of a city where she has lived her once bubbly

                life. The Walgreens is closing and the schools
            are broken down in this old neighborhood.
        Daily, I remember no one will be left to ask
     the things unknown to me. The staff smoke at the back
entrance. Past the storage trailers and the dumpsters

they can see the river, watch for the swell of wings
        cambered and primeval as dust, drowsy as time.
            I lift myself to see one, before I hold my breath
                and make myself dash inside, sprinting
                    the hallway past the sunroom and laundry,

                gliding the corners into her room, a dim landing.
            I let go my breath and cross to the window
        just in time to see the heron's dowel legs dangling,
     feathers cupped in ancient arc, neck folded
as an *S* ascending in resolve back to the rookery.

Gallows Humor

I cut my mother's curtains off the rods
with the same dressmaker's shears she had used
to slice the fabric from the bolt thirty
years before. Her steady zizz of steel through
cloth had once filled our closets with garments
of her making, had once dressed our windows
with lined linen panels and modest sheers.
My father's installation of the rods
was a gibbet meant to hold. I couldn't
tear them down so I climbed the ladder, cut
loose the drapes and watched them shudder and drop.
My parents were like this: fashioned
to endure, stubborn as an old post.

Sevens

My friend claims she saw her mom
skipping away to heaven
right after she died. I did
not see mine dance, though her voice
follows me around her house
as I shovel out her things—
Don't touch that. I need that. Please.

Paralysis

In my dreams my parents can always walk
unattended. No wheelchairs banging into walls,
no dead limbs heavier than the weight of the world.

My father takes an incline at a trot. He is on a mission
to fix somebody's washing machine, his toolbox
swinging light as a dinner pail. The zeal
of his stride makes my dream legs ache.

My mother dances around the sewing notions
on her dining room table, Ray Charles on the stereo,
unbolts layers of creamy taffeta across the living
room floor, stumps on her knees to pin the pattern,
cuts and sews a bridesmaid's dress in an afternoon.

In the evening my father climbs the ladder to the attic
while my mother below wrestles Aunt Ala's old walker
to hoist up to him. He stores it between the joists,
caged protector held in the hot darkness just in case.

My Maternal People

In my mama's photos they stare out directly, uncompromising....
I thought them beautiful and frightening.
   Dorothy Allison, *Two or Three Things I Know for Sure*

My maternal people are short and stout, thick-waisted
with unshapely legs and ankles like blocks. In a silent
home movie the camera pans around the circle
of women sitting in lawn chairs in the yard. They wear
dresses—short-sleeved shirtwaists with matching
fabric belts that sit right under their ample bosoms.
Their bellies round out softly like rising dough.
My maternal people never wore shorts or pants.

    Some don aprons because they must move
in and out of the hot kitchen, bringing food to men
or to children, who are in other circles. When they talk,
my maternal people wave their heavy arms loudly,
hefty punctuations signaling a punchline. Their hands
are veined arrows, always pointing the right way.

Kitchen Waltz

Here is the kettle and here is the spoon
A full moon in daylight splinters the sky
My mother is dead, my father, too
Their plots are quadrangles crooked and slumped

Here is the skillet, a halo of iron
A hundred years' worth of hands have heaved
It from the sizzling fires, cornbread and grease
And tedious days of crossing the floors

To cook and feed and wipe the board dry
Here is the basin and here is the rag
Here is the sorrow of hot soapy water
Chafing the wrists and blistering the heart

Tree Rings

When they meet me in my dreams, I do
what they say. We are encircled now, all

living together, my grandmothers and me.
Down dim paneled hallways I follow obediently

behind them. I answer their telephones in knotty
pine nooks. Those black eyes know

me. I hear their boarders walking over
our heads and I'm sent up the mahogany stair

case to collect the rent. I stand at the oak
door and knock. We are willow and birch,

enchanted and renewed; apple and blackthorn
blossoms with sharp spines. We are older

than the bristle cone pine in the desert. We are
the crone living in the elderberry shrub, straggly

and unruly in old age. We can grow anywhere,
conjuring, avenging, punishing.

We are the yew, adored above all others, screening
the doorway between this life and the next.

Ballad

Sycamores jut above a daybreak wet
with steam. The groundhogs are making

coffee. The heron flies above the tree
line, drumstick legs stretched rigid,

wing-flap on the upbeat like a crooked
song wounding the sky.

A family of house finches makes a dust bath
in the gravels at the end of my driveway.

They strum and pluck every shimmering
day while the worm entombs, while the bud

weeps on the vine. I've been broadcasting
seed in memoriam: my mother loved the killdeer,

her mother despised the bluejay,
the melancholy of its cries like a wretched

old love song hummed over and again.

To Sing and Sing Again

The sky is feathered with pewter
like the tail-wings of the bluejay
at the feeder. His magnificent scream
pierces the quiet of morning.

Praise his siren song, beckoning
a swirl of blue to the feeder: *Come
and be fed.* Soon wrens bob and peck
around the jays in harmony.

Praise be the squirrel who bosses
this feeder—sly chameleon
vanishing into the bare maple
limbs, reappearing in time

to battle a half-dozen crows,
those robed magistrates
of greed. Praise their black
surging and sassing on takeoff.

Praise the red-footed mourning
dove partners who bring
their young in at dusk, accept
the remains discarded by others.

Praise their meager ways,
the sad flutter of their leaving.
Praise the watchful redbird
who feeds first, alone, then

the females who feed together.
Praise mother and child I find
on the porch, a festival of red
feathers announcing a cat's

hidden perch. Praise the shovel
I use to lift them up. Praise their
rotting bodies nourishing the
woodsy earth, the pines full of nests.

The Chief Things of the Ancient Mountains

*Blessed . . . be his land . . . for the precious fruits brought forth by the sun,
and for the precious things put forth by the moon. And for the chief things
of the ancient mountains, and for the precious things of the lasting hills.*
    Deuteronomy 33:13–15

A boy who runs the creekbeds in his youth
grows up to see a stream with doubtful eyes,

suspects the worst to wash down from the mines,
follows his hope for work that puts it right.

A boy who plays in woods along the ridge
can't help but turn the chests of beech and oak

into tales where words stand straighter than
the copse of tulip poplars on the rise.

A boy who rests his head down in a field
sees clouds that stretch past his understanding,

aligns himself to mystery and trusts
that falling through blue dreams is not failing.

A boy who hears the brightest songs of birds
in morning when the sunball buffs the sky

believes a melody will bear all misery
and mark his days with questions and surprise.

The Full Corn Moon

They say those birthed during its fullness
are charmed. While we admire Fruit Moon,
Corn Moon, Barley Moon—the names

for its roundness this September night—
another side of the world celebrates
Worm Moon, Lenten Moon, Crow

Moon, Sugar Moon, Chaste Moon.
The charms of the moon, I cannot fathom—
how its face is lit in full sun when our paths

are dark; how the full moon and sun pool
their gravitational magic to make spring high
tides, no matter the season, how the moon

circles us but hides its far side; how the full
moon rises tonight and washes the trees
with shadows. *Dulisdi*, Nut Moon, say

the Cherokee. Pawpaw Moon, say the Shawnee.
Moon When the Plums Are Scarlet, Moon
When the Deer Paw the Earth, Moon

When the Calves Grow Hair, say those
in the Plains. Tonight in Kentucky, a phase
of bounty, of winnowing and reaping.

Gravity Sonnet

Drowsing, I hear her yipping dream, feel
her climbing my hip through rhythmic breaths.
She is my squirrel dog who can't hunt, fretful
and brain-hurt from seizures I ease with Valium
and Phenobarbital. The vet told me mountain
men hunting bear would send in their little
feists like her to *worry* the bear so they could
come in with their big dogs for the kill.

Here each night her deep sleep is what keeps
the mauling away. When the house is still
and receptive to ghosts, she burrows
in blankets, stretches out long, syncs
with the night's measure and pulls
with the moon, a washing over our sleep.

Roll Call (A Dissimulation of Birds)

Goldfinch: The Acrobat

yellow charms flicker as heartbeats
around the thistle-sock trapeze
flying circus for just a blink

Cowbird: The Malefactor

gimcrack work-shy thieving outlaw
vengeance teeming jagged raucous
dark-eyed homewrecker on the draw

Tufted Titmouse: The Constable

topknotted peewee high sheriff
homeguard of the pignut hickory
whistleblower *chirrup! chirrup!*

Mourning Dove: The Saint

red-footed peacenik murmuring
lamentations for us pleading
squab of mercy interceding

Bluejay: The Mercenary

belted down in pewter and smart
cobalt vesture crested marauder
warehousing swag lookout guarding

Mockingbird: The Ballad Collector

sings by ear polyglot preacher
moonlit dancer fierce tune jumper
thrice-turned phrases old song catcher

Killdeer: The Player

chattering plover broken-wing
acts as double-cross marooning
on dry land hit the ground running

Crow: The Trickster

hollering gang of lousy kids
snooping club-footed delinquents
coursing the roads charges dismissed

Lone Crow Daddy Spends
His Afternoon Setting Up a Carnival

Then the crows turned their voices to great rejoicing
New York Times, 1884

Lone Crow Daddy commands the highest pitch
of my roof and the mockingbirds are pissed.

Crow Daddy hops the roofline
      unfazed, so urbane,
taking his sweet time. He flaps

to the ground toward the woods, a sough
of wind in the grasses. From the sycamore

boughs he telegraphs his version of the story
      across the fowl riot of mockingbirds.
Robins come scrapping and bluejays screech

in to boss the job. Meanwhile, under attack,
Lone Crow Daddy glides over to the high

pitch of my neighbor's roof. Ignores
      his critics. He lifts a wing in preening,
departs for the next roofline. Only now do I realize

his game. I think about the poet who warned
me of my *disingenuous tendency* to give human

qualities to the animals in my poems. *Fuck him,*
      Crow Daddy would say.
Days later five crows have set up shop with Lone Crow

Daddy, holding auditions for ringmaster
in these bawling neighborhood skies.

Small-Town Gossip

The best place to hear it? Not in the beauty shop, that warren
of backcombing and flaming hearsay; nor the church house

where prayer requests stand in for scandal. Do not listen
for it in the garages where men gather by twos and threes

gripping their coffee cups and old grudges; or in the Dollar
Store where old couples block the aisles comparing

ailments and dog-tired young women run in for cheap diapers
while their men wait for them, smoking, in idling cars.

You won't hear it the grocery store either, as aggravated
shoppers fume into their phones while stalking the aisles.

The best place—just listen—the best place is before good
daylight when the mockingbird practices his scales,

when the redbirds wake and cheer each other to the day's work:
chipping seed, ignoring the propaganda of jaybirds and crows.

My Grandmother's Dog Song

Honey, her tits were all but dragging the ground.
She came loping down the mountain and took

the road at a trot. She had pups somewhere
I figured and was hunting her a rabbit. I whistled

but she shortcutted back up into the woods.
Next day, she inched a little closer but when I called,

just as soft as a biddy, she turned tail and scratched up
the ridge. Now tomorrow, we'll see how she likes a song.

Do you know this one? *Old yeller dog come trotting
through the meeting house way down in Alabam . . .*

Bounty

In the dewy morning the cucumbers
you twisted from prickly garden vines

will darken and crisp on your yellow
kitchen table, preserving a memory

of tendrils crawling through wormy soil
and the broad leaves that canopied

them in the heated day. They remember
stretching from melon flowers. They

remember the bees who sugared
the stigma. Their seeds will tell you a story

of sowing and reaping, a tale suspended
in jelly, recited in your salads, read

in the Benedictine spread on your bread,
and tasted in an emerald grace.

Barn Swallows

Little fighter-pilot parents swoop
into their nest three stories

high in the hospital breezeway.
A chalice of gob and mud

atop the sprinkler-head cups,
tiny ostomies of endless hungers.

Scissor tails swallow the air, clipping,
clipping. What are the questions

I should be asking here as droppings
mound up on the concrete steps

around my feet like splotched offerings?

Put Upon by Grief

My dead! I miss you! Won't you give a sign?
Make a joke at my expense?
  Robin Becker, "In Montefiore Cemetery"

Send us a feather, like the woman
who in her worst sorrow begged
for a gesture from her beloved dead
and a velvet wisp of wing floated
right down to her lap. So the story
goes—but we have quit believing.

Our traumas have been too brutal.
We stand beat up and bruised. Starlings
have hijacked our trees. Now
the quarrel songs of crows and jays rout
from the next ridge. Now the woodpeckers
hammer in less hateful climes. Only
mockingbirds appear at ease.

Now the unpacking and repacking.
Now the stacking or hauling away.
At dusk bats plunge into our garages
and can't find the way out. House wrens
foul our storage boxes with their grassy
bowls, their eggs spotted as rotting grapes.

Now comes the sweating through
a full-tilt panic. Now is the shattering
of our unfolding and breaking open.

The hawk hunts in our ditches then hurtles
headfirst into our walls. And the glory
of it all flutters past us. We miss
it and are foregone. Send us a feather.

Gospel Song

When the Cooper's hawk slammed into the corner
wall I thought the neighbor boys had thrown a baseball
at the house. In my rush to chase down those kids
I nearly missed his ringed tail, his speckled breast
that looked for all the world like a designer cable-knit
sweater, how he looked for all the world like he was
just tucked down for a nap, his neck bent just so.

Every day since, I've yearned to find a wonder
in my yard, a wish for personal salvation.

Each morning my friend remembers a hymn to sing aloud
while she waits for the coffee to piss into her cup. Keurig
hymns, she calls them. If gospel songs are all that remain
of my childhood dogma, can I still be saved,
even if the creeds still slink around after me sometimes?

I don't know. Isn't dread now marking my dark
path that leads to the forest where I bury the hawk?

The woods at the edge of my yard shelter rowdy birds
who like to fight and holler, their chatter like gunfire.
Even the tiny wren, so fierce in her competitions, built
and rejected three nests in my garage: one in a snow
boot, one in the toolbox, one behind the paint cans.
I stay out of her way and try to ignore the blue-tailed
skinks who colonize the cracks along the driveway.

Sorrow Lets Loose for a Moment

Sure-footed already, three fawns scale
the bank at the hairpin
twist on Old Corbin Pike. Early

haze spots the morning as I brake
at the dead
man's curve, the forest
floor below us abysmal,
a burial garment.

We all stop   —quaver,
bolt   & lift.

Offal & Bones

Then one unto the other said
Where shall we go and dine today?
   "The Twa Corbies," Scottish ballad

Two buzzards roost on either side
of the Hartsville Pike exit sign
hanging across the interstate.
An image so symmetrical

it's sinister. You rush to make
sense of two buzzards dreamily
centered over the expressway.
It's deeply comic, a gimmick,
you think, a billboard hawking some
backwoodsy diner. Heckle & Jeckle
as squawking hillbilly mascots.

Or, it's the opening edit
of a Stanley Kubrick movie,
the looming establishing shot,
the camera pulling in slow, dragged
down by a Ligeti soundtrack.
(Oh György, such dread foreboding
in music unhinged from the rules!)

It's a bad omen, rotten luck,
a jinx foretold to drive under
them at seventy miles an hour.
You fear you'll crash through some portal
smeared with pitch and briers. You just know—
when you check the rearview mirror

before the tar-hole closes like
an iris wipe behind you—those
buzzards will be hissing at you.

Oh, Groundhog!

Rodent just means its teeth never stop
growing, my friend tells me when I confess
my obsession for the groundhog who has moved
in next door. But groundhog is kin to squirrel
and rat, is *rodent*, is greasy, ferocious of tooth,
is hated by my ancestors, farmers all.

Oh, groundhog! the consonants click in all
your nicknames. I say them aloud
from my kitchen window to conjure you:
whistle-pig
      land beaver
            ground pig
                  thickwood badger
                      red monk
                           woodchuck

I admire his waddle, his fur the color of rotting
wood, out early in the morning, getting fatter
and fatter on the endless
salad bar that is my neighbor's abandoned yard.
His ears are wispy cups of velvet, upright in relief
to the gray frost of the guard hairs curving
his spine. When he stands up to spy
for my dog, he is the effigy of silence, unsocial.
Yet, in the late evening at second feeding, he grazes
unafraid while the neighborhood calico rests next
to him in the clover and trumpet creeper. *He eats
till his britches won't button at all.*

Oh, groundhog! You are all I want. Let me
eat all summer. Let me burrow. Let me hide.
Let my body fevers drop to sleep in the cool
chambered heart of your tunnels. Let me mark
my own shadow to forecast the springtide
and wake to daffodils rippling.

Let me have teeth
of the rodent to bite through this world.

Mapmaker

The map is not the territory. The word is not the thing.
   Alfred Korzybski

Do you see those black oaks on the ridge?
Remember to look up each time you pass under.

Hunger how to mark them on the page. Wonder
if their shadows ever change. Can you graph

their scaly nutshells, draw a pattern of the leaves
while they fall? As the jaybird builds her nest

in its branches, listen for the siren of your name.
When you set off for its roots, are you worried

that the lonesome trail you're walking has no end?
With your boots, toe a line of memory;

with your knife, carve your name. Chart how
it is to cut the heartwood. Will the cords you stack

keep you warm? Does a word plotted in the wind
please you? Please sketch a map that we can sing.

Notes and Acknowledgments

The italicized passage in "Rank Stranger" is from poet Louise McNeill's memoir, *The Milkweed Ladies* (University of Pittsburgh Press, 1988).

"A. P. Carter v. Sara Cater, 1932" is a contrapuntal poem, particularly inspired by Tyehimba Jess's *Leadbelly* (Wave Books, 2005).

"Knoxville Boy" borrows lyrics from two songs: "Knoxville Girl" and "Edward" (Child Ballad #13).

"Recitatives on a Murder" is based on the many legends of Tom Dula, but mostly inspired by a haunting I've had since I was a little girl when I heard Doc Watson's recording of "Tom Dooley" and read the liner notes on my mother's copy of his debut recording for Vanguard Records in 1964. Watson's great-grandmother Betsy Triplett Watson had tended to Ann Foster Melton on her deathbed and recalled that Ann Melton claimed "she could see the flames of Hell at the foot of her bed."

"The Girl Singer" borrows lyrics from these songs: "Dreadful Wind and Rain," "The Twa Sisters" (Child Ballad #10), "Pretty Polly," "The Cuckoo Bird," and "Omie Wise."

"Barn Dance (Costume)" was inspired by lyrics from two songs: "Been All Around This World" and "Katy Cruel."

"Barn Dance (Chorus)" uses the actual stage names of early female performers of county music, often assigned to them by their male managers.

"Maybelle Carter on Singing Hillbilly Boogie with Sara, ca. 1963" quotes the lyrics from "I'm Leaving You (This Lonesome Song)," written by Alton and Rabon Delmore.

"On Seeing a Letter Patsy Cline Wrote to Nudie the Tailor" uses the words from Cline's actual letter, received on March 6, 1963, and exhibited as part of *Sparkle & Twang: Marty Stuart's American Music Odyssey* (Tennessee State Museum, 2007).

"I Will Always Love You" takes its title from the Dolly Parton song.

The italicized couplet in "Pentecost 1965" is from Acts 2:1, King James Bible.

"James Brown Performs 'Cold Sweat' on *American Bandstand*, 1968" quotes lyrics from "Cold Sweat" by James Brown.

"My Grandmother's Dog Song" quotes lyrics from "Old Yeller Dog (Come Trottin' Through the Meeting House)," a variant of a nineteenth-century minstrel song.

"Oh, Groundhog!" takes its title and borrows a line from the traditional folksong of the same name.

Many kind thanks to the editors of the publications where these poems were published, some in slightly different form:

94 Creations, "A. P. Carter v. Sara Carter, 1932," "On Seeing a Letter Patsy Cline Wrote to Nudie the Tailor"
ABZ: A Poetry Magazine, "The Girl Singer"
American Society: What Poets See, "Rebel Girl (Hazel Dickens)"
Anthology of Appalachian Writers XIII, "My Maternal People"
Appalachian Review, "I saw Bobby Bare kiss Marty Stuart," "James Brown Performs 'Cold Sweat' on *American Bandstand*, 1968," "War Story" (as "Photograph")
Artists Thrive, "The Full Corn Moon"
Bigger Than They Appear, "Thanksgiving Eve"
Birmingham Arts Journal, "Corvus"
Change Seven, "Gospel Song," "Gravity Sonnet," "Vocal School"
Clapboard House, "Minor Detour through an Old Knoxville Neighborhood"
Grist, "Kitchen Waltz" (as "Failed Meal")
Flycatcher, "Rank Stranger" (as "Voyager")
HeartWood, "Small-Town Gossip"
HillVille, "Pentecost 1965"
Journal of Kentucky Studies, "Maybelle Carter on Singing Hillbilly Boogie with Sara, ca. 1963"
Kudzu, "Barn Dance (Costume)," "Herons on the Holston," "I Will Always Love You," "Index of Canticles," "Knoxville Boy," "Lone Crow Daddy Spends His Afternoon Setting Up a Carnival," "My Grandmother's Dog Song," "Offal & Bones," "Put Upon by Grief," "Roll Call"
Larger Bodies Than Mine, "Tree Rings"
New Southerner, "To Sing and Sing Again"
Outscape: Writings on Fences and Frontiers, "Mapmaker"

Pikeville Review, "Barn Dance (Road Show)," "Gallows Humor"

Pine Mountain Sand & Gavel, "The Chief Things of the Ancient Mountains," "Dead Man's Tuning," "Sevens"

pluck! The Journal of Affrilachian Arts & Culture, "My Grandmother's Sewing Notions"

See How We Are, "Poem in My Grandmother's Voice"

Shaking Like a Mountain, "Recitatives on a Murder"

Shenandoah, "Slow Dance"

Southern Poetry Anthology: Tennessee, "Paralysis"

Talking River, "Ballad," "Barn Swallows," "Sorrow Lets Loose for a Moment"

A Tapestry of Voices, "Barn Dance (Chorus)," "Barn Dance (Cousin Emmy Remembers Her Show Car")

Vinegar & Char: Verse from the Southern Foodways Alliance, "Bounty"

Wind, "Love in the Cold War"

Many generous friends and organizations helped me with these poems, and I am grateful for all of them. The list is too long to name here, but it really does take a village (and a whole heap of writing classes and workshops).

Thanks especially to my first college poetry teacher, Jeff Daniel Marion, who believed in me from the start and remained my friend for nearly four decades. Rest in peace, Danny.

I'm indebted to two of the smartest poets I know, who read this manuscript in its early stages and gave me valuable help in shaping it: Rebecca Gayle Howell and William Wright.

I'm grateful for my editor in this project, my friend and colleague Silas House.

I'm beholden to the hard work of the very best people at Fireside Industries/ University Press of Kentucky.

Special love and thanks to Alice Hale Adams, Nickole Brown, Peter Cooper, Jackie White Crosslin, Laura Dennis, Sam Gleaves, Jesse Graves, Becky Hamilton, Pauletta Hansel, Caroline Herring, Ron Houchin, Jason Howard, Leatha Kendrick, Sonja Livingston, George Ella Lyon, Maurice Manning, Greta McDonough, Daniel Martin Moore, RB Morris, Josh Mullins, Beth Newberry, Harry Rice, Savannah Sipple, Jamey Hill Temple, Lyrae Van Clief-Stefanon, Doug Van Gundy, Frank X Walker, Kathi Whitley, Crystal Wilkinson, and Cyndi Williams.

I am thankful for the support I received from the Berea College Appalachian Sound Archives Fellowship Program, the Hindman Settlement School, the Kentucky Arts Council, and the Kentucky Foundation for Women.

"Ballad" is for Rebecca Gayle Howell.

"Bounty" and "The Chief Things of the Ancient Mountains" are for Silas House.

"Mapmaker" is for Maurice Manning.

"Offal & Bones" is for Keith Semmel.

About the Author

Marianne Worthington is cofounder and poetry editor of *Still: The Journal*, an online literary magazine publishing writers, artists, and musicians with ties to Appalachia since 2009. Her work has appeared in *Oxford American, CALYX, Grist, Shenandoah, Cheap Pop, Chapter 16*, and *Vinegar and Char: Verse from the Southern Foodways Alliance*, among other places. She received the Al Smith Fellowship from the Kentucky Arts Council and artist grants from the Kentucky Foundation for Women and the Berea College Appalachian Sound Archives Fellowship Program. She has edited four literary anthologies, most recently *Piano in a Sycamore: Writing Lessons from the Appalachian Writers' Workshop*, coedited with Silas House. She grew up in Knoxville, Tennessee, and lives, writes, and teaches in southeast Kentucky.

1/22